GW01339894

ASSARACUS

A JOURNAL OF GAY POETRY
ISSUE 07

SiblingRivalryPress
ALEXANDER, ARKANSAS
WWW.SIBLINGRIVALRYPRESS.COM

Assaracus
A Journal of Gay Poetry
Issue 7: July 2012
ISBN: 978-1-937420-21-5
ISSN: 2159-0478
Bryan Borland, Editor
Brent Calderwood, Associate Editor
Philip F. Clark, Art Editor
Copyright © 2012 by Sibling Rivalry Press

Cover Photograph Donated by Trent Kelley, Curator of "Hidden in the Open." Used by Permission.

All rights reserved. No part of this journal may be reproduced or republished without written consent from the publisher, except by reviewers who may quote brief excerpts in connection with a review in a newspaper, magazine, or electronic publication; nor may any part of this journal be reproduced, stored in a retrieval system, or transmitted in any form without written consent of the publisher. However, contributors maintain ownership rights of their individual poems and as such retain all rights to publish and republish their work.

Sibling Rivalry Press, LLC
13913 Magnolia Glen Drive
Alexander, AR 72002

www.siblingrivalrypress.com
info@siblingrivalrypress.com

Assaracus Issue 07

The Poems of Jonathan Bracker
p. 7

The Poems of Jason Contrucci
p. 18

The Poems of Sebastian Doherty
p. 27

The Poems of David Keali'i
p. 38

The Poems of Dean Kostos
p. 49

The Poems of Anthony Lioi
p. 63

The Poems of Philip Matthews
p. 77

The Poems of Ian James Morgan
p. 87

The Poems of Stephen Potter
p. 97

The Poems of Patrick Stevens
p. 109

The Poems of Peter Weltner
p. 119

Featuring Art Donated by Trent Kelley
About the Collection p. 134

JONATHAN BRACKER

REPLACING THE RECEIVER

JONATHAN BRACKER was born in New York City in 1936. His collections of poems are: *Constellations Of Clover* (Prickly Pear Press, 1973); *Duplicate Keys* (Thorp Springs Press, 1977); *Some Poems About Women* (Bootleg Press, 1993); *Paris Sketches* (Thorp Spring Press, 2005); and *Civilian Aboard U. S. Navy Ship At Sea* (Seven Kitchens Press, 2011). Poems included here have previously appeared in *Off the Rocks*, *The New Yorker*, and *Poetry Northwest*. Jonathan has lived in San Francisco since 1973.

LOVE POEM NUMBER GOD KNOWS WHAT

> *"There are moments when everything turns out right.*
> *Don't let it alarm you; they pass."*
> — Jules Renard, Journal

The longer I know you
The more
I think I may be
Going sane.

For instance: when I visit this afternoon,
A large slim youthful dog ambles over to lick
Not too wetly my delighted ear,
Reducing me to a ducking, grinning boy.

Sunlight through high windows
Massages my head as I fit in your sofa's curve,
Borzoi unmoving for the moment so fingers can twine
His dry curly hair like a field of white hyacinths.

A Schubert trio on the stereo, and milky, honeyed tea;
Not talk but a conversation occurs.
Then Max pads to find his leash to take us
For our exercise. Climbing Alamo Park's gentle hill with you

Past reaching trees and gardener-bedded flowers
I forget my complaints of sirens, screams in the night,
Beggars seemingly everywhere, abrupt confrontations,
Refuse blown across my walking feet.

They say happiness cannot be known in the moment;
They are wrong.
Just now, I cannot condemn or fear. If I can only somehow continue
Losing my mind!

WE CALL EACH OTHER NOW, TO NOT COMPLAIN

We call each other now, to not complain.
At nine o'clock or soon after, most mornings,
One of us telephones. Our conversation consists

Mainly of books we read, movies we see,
Music we are listening to, for we are in our seventies
And over the last thirty years have complained

Enough to sufficiently annoy each other;
We're over that now, and seldom discuss
Emotional well-being, fear, worry, or religion

Any more. I have never visited my friend
In his Tenderloin hotel room on the seventh floor,
Because of my anxiety in elevators; now, walking up

Is out of the question. He says he does not mind.
We meet each month for coffee; sometimes he comes
To my rent-controlled apartment for lunch and to pet my cat.

Aware that our mornings can be quite difficult even if sleep
Has been deep and dreamless, before replacing the receiver
One of us usually thanks the other, for being there.

AT SEVENTY, FROM A PARK BENCH

Undistinguished old dandelion!
Your yellow is predictably
Only the color of scrambled eggs.
Your fringe-petals have become tacky.
You are merely like a little stilled hedgehog.

Now though a robin alertly hops by
Somehow its beak is not yellow—
And the color of its breast and stomach
Is merely the color of those four fallen leaves
Covered and uncovered by wind-stirred tree-branch shadows.
Taller than grassblades, little white daisies reach;

An unmoving beetle's copper body kindles in sunlight;
A black fly making ablutions on my light-grey shirt
Disappears the moment I shift. Now I recall
Dandelions like large-headed mushrooms
Fork-lifted by young children.

TREES

So greatly that I hardly see them, trees
Intimidate. (I know the names of flowers,
Not of trees.)

Exceedingly over my head, standing so forthright
They are no one person's
Birthright,

Trees loom or lift and are not shaken by showers
To bend and patronize me,
As I do flowers.

Having enough to raise without raising objections,
They war only within themselves,
Their sections

Dipping to each other like professors at a meeting.
This is their only breach of the peace
And greeting.

OPPOSITES OF STRAIGHT

Curving, bending.

Not: *queer, crooked, wayward, out-of-joint,*
Gnarled, wizened, bandy, bowed,
Crippled, snaking, knock-kneed, askew,
Maimed, deviating, knurled–

But antlers
Disclosed by
Lightning,

The dragonfly, his zigzag hovering,
Twigs rafted on a stream,
The tacking advent of swans toward hand-held offerings.
The ins-and-outs of hummingbirds. Pigeons' progress. Some
Bills, legs, unfolding wings (and the unfolded legs of cats),
The necks of birds (the darter's thrust, the heron's
Upward toss to order fish), how sandpipers spirt
Across blotting sand.

The investigatory spider's light approach.
Ligament, filament.
Eyelid, -brow and -lash. The wrists.
Now-pulsing blood through arteries.
Pastern, fetlock, hoof. Rootlets. And trees.
The raindrop's slow successive downpane path. Paths.
Peaks. Eagles'
Outings.

All burgeonings: the sweet-pea tendril's grasp; unsmooth
Viny wood from which wisteria-blossoms grape;
Petunia seedlings, their green slight shoulder-pads fronding
Into strength. Worm-tunnelings. The in-
Direction of an ant. Garter snakes' naive appearances. Dark
Skittery flies. Grasshopper-leaps,
Grasshopper-flights.

The prickly meadow grass, the manly weeds to stretch and laugh out on
Beneath the sheer and unpolemic sky sky-blue and gay.

JUNIOR HIGH: BOHEMIAN LIFE

The boy loved to go to the all-music store (he could explore the new invention,
Long-playing records, at Sears Roebuck also, but here were listening booths
And diamond needles, and wide aisles for studying the words on the standard
Paper sleeves of singles: a white Greek column top tilted against blue sky)—

That is, until the day he saw standing with the studious mustached owner
A burly man like an auto mechanic, wearing a starched clean grey-blue jump suit
Open to a thick belt: all the way to the navel, curly black hair against pale skin.
The two adult males seemed easy with each other. The boy's heart beat

Uncomfortably fast. Another world intruded into this air-conditioned place where he
Had felt so safe. Twisting to look at something pointed out, the man revealed more chest.
Almost a nipple. Shocked, the boy slipped awkwardly past to finger through other bins,
Considering never returning, rather than risking seeing such things again.

(What he did not know was that Septimus, who looked as though he smoked cigars,
Had lived with his old-world mother in a large house with a lovingly tended rose garden
Until the age of thirty-six when he built himself a cottage in which to live alone,
A cottage large enough to have friends over as often as he wished, sometimes listening

With them to Andre Kostelanetz' Jerome Kern Favorites, a boxed set whose cover art
Showed a stave of music bending in and out as in a Walt Disney featurette:
Cheerful large black notes high and low all down its lines,
Poised like perching birds.)

JUNIOR HIGH: AT AN END OF THE FIELD

Six of them did not play sports. At P. E. they stood about,
Together trying for nonchalance, speaking a bit with eyes downcast
While behind and around them boys thundered like buffaloes.

Giraffes is what they were. Bert Adkins gingerly scuffed his new sneakers
In playground dust while Larry Bernard told really quite odd jokes;
Bob Sakowitz fidgeting the hem of his too-tight regulation gym shorts

Made at least one of them uneasy. These young men were hoping
No ball would hit them hard or land at their feet and need to be scooped up
And returned in a masculine manner. Surprisingly, no coach dispersed their circle.

They were impossible, it was simply that. Though four had begun to see
How being now unlike others might help a boy succeed as an adult,
Looking barely content they all had sunburnt ears cocked for the ending bell.

JUNIOR HIGH: ONCE DURING P.E.

Melee in the shower area, the boy only hears.
From the bench where he hotly bends to lace
His Buster Browns, out of the corner of an eye
Seeing naked or towel-waisted boys slip around the corner
To an echoing space of dangerous jostlings on wet tile,
Joyous screams, loud exclamations, and breathless waitings
For the inevitable arrival of Coach to put a stop to this,
He knows he must quickly empty his locker and bolt
Up the stairs to a hallway and its classrooms.

Yet what has never happened before (to his inexact knowledge)
Seems not terrible, though no boy will tell a mother.

Forever he will wish he had gone to stand unobserved
Outside the outer ring of spectators, to see.

JUNIOR HIGH: FOUND OUT

Often when they are there, stretching over his sister's bed upstairs in back
He lifts a venetian slat to peer at Tom Lovell and Tom's gang
Escaping, feinting, twisting—some shirtless—before their garage hoop.

Today after school they are absent. Sprawling, he reads Carson McCullers,
First peeling back the spread so the corduroy will not get creased
(His mother insists on this); across the hall she sits at an easel
Tediously drawing a rich person's portrait for rent money.

Daddy is gone from the apartment, Sis out with an athletic girl friend.
In May's heat the boy begins to doze. Suddenly up the street out front
An open convertible's racket explodes and the startling honk of its horn,

With young males in it whom he cannot see but knows are Lovell's buddies
Loudly shouting a truth about him which half the street can hear,
Broadcasting his name—his first name and his last—
Then yelling in one word their comprehension of what he is.

This is like his Shreveport nightmares during World War II
In which the boy saw Hitler's planes repeatedly strafe ghettos.
Wondering who is old enough to actually drive the long yellow car,

His heart painfully pounding, the boy horrors only
"She heard it! She had to hear it! There is no way
She cannot have heard it!" And then, "A hateful thing to do!"
Followed by "The dreadful thing about it, it is true."

After that, six hours internally cowering, almost slinking, slowly waiting
For something distressing to be done or said. But Daddy comes home
And he is not taken behind any closed door. The boy begins to know

This will become something else they need not talk about. Enduring dinner,
Eating very little, falling asleep at two in the morning after jerking and twitching
And clutching at moist sheets, he shows up next day at school
Where from eight to three he is fearful, concerned where he places his eyes.

SYSTEMATIC

The graveyard is God's file
For future reference,
With tombstone tabs the wind thumbs through,
Indexing accounts the grass has closed.

THE BURNING-GLASS

Perhaps the sun
Consists of golden moths.

Something has eaten holes
In the rugs of shade
Thrown by the trees
On the floor of the woods.

JASON CONTRUCCI

SURVIVAL SEX

JASON CONTRUCCI studied poetry at the University of Michigan. After six years as a proposal writer in New York City, he returned to Ann Arbor where he literally lives on Easy Street but in fact tries very hard. He has worked at the University of Michigan Press since 2007 and has volunteered teaching writing workshops through 826michigan.

ABDUCTED

I know what they're thinking—Nice muffin top.
Balances the plump heart surgery scar, gray chest
hairs, wispy comb-over exposed: not 'receding'
but 'bald.' Those broken capillaries of nightly
martinis the wife started counting aloud;
resentment of technology, ever over or
under-exuberant sexual performance, lack
of imagination even to have believed
in aliens—Who do they think they are?
So goddamned superior, all silver skin and
bones; enormous top-heavy craniums,
steely sexless torsos, that effeminate
clucking. Naked as I and without being
belted to a metal slab under floodlights.
At least I think they're naked.

BIOSPHERE 2

Whether it's the air thinning on the savannah
or our nutrient-stuffed diet, if I have to hear
Terry read me one more "log" entry or lecture
on the *psycho-spiritual* imbalance of gases
carbon and oxygen that silenced the pollinating
insects and left one doomed pygmy goat, I'll
toss him in the mangrove swamp before every
eighty-dollar tourist smudging the glass
however earth-shattering the survival sex
or badly we need him to hold off Doc Adams'
tribe for 18 months more. At least I hope someone
spies us making up all over the rain forest.

THE END IS HERE

For months now, the Seventh-Day Adventists at the end
of our street were getting carried away with the sign in
the church lawn. The block letters only ever spelled out
the worship times when the late service dropped off, replaced by
WITH GOD ALL THINGS ARE POSSIBLE or like biblical
slogan as nostalgic as the tan brick with disco shades
of geometric stained glass. Then the bumper sticker
humor took over, fitfully at first and often signed
as in DON'T MAKE ME COME DOWN THERE –GOD
until it was all divine comedy casting the
Almighty as harried parent, middle management,
which swiftly turned to the clever condescension of
SALVATION GUARANTEED OR MISERY REFUNDED
and soon no service times at all in favor of smarmy,
longwinded remonstrances like 10 SUGGESTIONS? NO.
WHAT PART OF THOU SHALT NOT DON'T YOU UNDERSTAND.
The meanness darkened to outright condemnation and
the community became concerned. GO TO HELL
read the sign week before last BUT DON'T TAKE US WITH YOU,
and finally escalated to attacks on the
neighbors' teenage children too vulgar to repeat here.
Even so, the message this morning as I drove off to work
almost made me feel sorry for them: WHY GOD WHY,
one of the larger airborne beasts on patrol more and more lately
coiled around their modest steeple with fire in its eyes like
it would incinerate anyone coming in or out.

TSUNAMI

"The death count rose to one hundred thousand today—"
That can't be right—This sleeve needs one more roll.
I don't take two hours a day in the gym
To let some mudslide upstage my mike bicep;
They can see mosquito bites through the face makeup.
"The death toll swelled to one hundred thousand even
As waters began to recede—" For three days a record
Twelve million have tuned into the devastation
Humidity reeks on *the* Ivy League crew cut.
"And the first wave of U.S. aid reached survivors."
Because of my rolling brow they watch, the trademark
Depths of my blue eyes, their watery light, the *anchor*:
"The deaths crested at a hundred thou—" Or is it
Twelve thousand victims, one hundred million viewers.

SWEET NOTHINGS IN THE YEAR 2135

A brain of egospheres anti-gravved in the dome
of the square, his own orb whooshing upward as Marc
joined the male personas lounging in plush stands below
where he shared rec periods profiling unfamiliars—

One down second over in the next stands.
His e-sphere urged first-person contact with the
redhead cadet exhaling from her vapo stem
(to aid unit cohesion), then came out of the cloud

of misty metal and glass, its screen tinted with his
and this "Marie's" G.R.I.D. of predeterminates versus
variables: she'll overlook his unequal physique,
see his lapses in cosmetic refining as evidence of

future stability, while her lack of living parents will
gel nicely with disdain for his own. Before leaving
she shifted seats to nuzzle his neck as he tongued
her wrist and above their tastes in pets were reconciled,

relative distances to quarters super-computed.
Marie's ego bobbed after her and his trailed last,
not returning till Marc's third try, reminding him to drink his
nanolytes if he wanted a better connection next time.

MR. SPACESHIP

Professor Thomas felt the titanium swell of his hull
and flexed lateral thrusters in turn listing port then
starboard at a cool clear burn. In fractions of thought
the Old Man flicked switches meant for index fingers,
sensed the whoosh of all-important air through opened
and closing weapons hatches into star-spangled void.
Deep within, the naked brain buzzed in its nutrient
tank of supercharged solution while console lights
winked their rhythmic red, blue and white status.
It felt good to be young again, too able-bodied to
return to naïve, war-happy scientists to say nothing
of his tender cargo, unwitting colonists for some far
planet where they three would start over at peace.

TO BE READ IN YOUR BEST TEXAS TWANG:

Mom says always wear a shirt to match the color of yer eyes for a first date and I'd have to agree. I'll never forget the first time Andrew Thornton noticed my eyes then kissed me on the cheek. I mean what guy kisses a girl on the cheek anymore? None far as I can tell, even if it is a nice date. But Drew did, tipped his pretend hat and said 'See ya 'round.' And I still have that shirt of Kimberly's that I's wearin' even though I had to tell her I lost it. She ain't ever gonna catch me cuz I only wear it for Drew 'n Drew's never around anymore. Mom says 'Why buy the cow when ya can get the milk for free.' Do all moms say that about the milk? Cuz it's real mean. Besides he says that ain't the reason, and I ain't no dairy cow. She's right about the shirt thing though. I just wish my eyes weren't so damned orange.

TECHNICAL DIFFICULTIES

They delivered the new TV before I woke up. Flipping through the channels, I thought I saw myself co-anchoring the news. When I switched back it was on to weather, but three clicks over, there I was in a commercial protesting that my cereal could be nutritious and taste this great. I found nothing in the manual left primly in the side drawer and at last phoned the hotline printed on the back cover. "Why yes, the latest models are fully self-programming," the consumer agent replied, mimicking my accent seamlessly. "I'm everyone," I insisted, clicking through me as the peppy yet tough prosecutor in last season's hit cop drama. "Change can be very disorienting," chirped the accused. "But I didn't order a new TV," I shouted, then softening in black and white opposite Brando on the street curb, "I've never even done any formal acting."

SEBASTIAN DOHERTY

THE DIFFICULTY OF PANTS

SEBASTIAN DOHERTY is the author of *The Real Donner Party*, a chapbook by the National Federation of State Poetry Societies. He was a 2010 fellow at the Bucknell Seminar for Younger Poets and attends Metropolitan State College of Denver, Colorado.

THE NIGHT DANCES
after Sylvia Plath

I danced in your vacant bedroom
    the night you went away

among the things you left behind
    and inexplicably:

the bottle of holy water
    with a cat sticker stuck

over the image of Jesus,
    the six unopened tubes

of chapstick on an empty shelf.
    I am a limp-wristed

firework in its warm spiral.
    Heaven's a human smell

bleeding its bright comets. I watch
    the extra space erase

itself, and emptied with my breath.
    I wear the memory

of you for a cold cross, glad for
    amnesias of a smile

which lay dropped in your unmade bed
    and irretrievable.

STRANGERS ON A TRAIN

Stranger on the train sits across from me.
My leg extends into the empty space
and up my inner thigh I find his knee,

though I'm pretending not to notice. He
looks at me in the window's angled trace.
Averting my gaze to the left, I see

a blind girl in our car speaking softly
to her guide dog. I glance back to his face
and feel the blindness whisper to my knee

for God on his behalf to intercede
with me. The train chugs at its constant pace
announcing each strange station may now be

the parting of us, or further, maybe,
parting of knees. The train has its odd chase
to make, encouraging beneath my knee

the meeting of my legs. Before I freed
myself, I came to the deciding place
with the stranger sitting across from me,
and gently took his hand above my knee.

THE RABBIT CATCHER
after Sylvia Plath

My hearth rugs pant, reclined near the plastic
patio furniture, save for the last:
small as a rabbit, the tight china barks,
as he goes hunting butterflies. The few

he catches in his mouth enter a red
vein stiffened filigree. I hate to watch
the glassy pangs of teeth, but I prefer
it to the sounds of you packing inside.

Suitcases with their finger snares snapped shut,
the wordless closures of malignity
filter through the yellow sliding-screen door.
You're leaving with the ringing force of tides

revolving on their turntable. Little
one catches his next prey. Sweethearts flutter
inside his mouth, stained glass as it shatters
with air through wings. Each one is slowly killed

with the patience needed for a violent
exorcism. I'm stoic at your smile.
Dull hands, blunt mouth, the walls move within me
to reveal my dark, empty hotel rooms.

The dogs get up to say goodbye. I sit
with my quiet cup of coffee, gagging
on a black zero shaped like a closing
throat or an insect's thin perforation.

FRIEND OF DOROTHY

At night I would clamber
into bed and curl up
next to her, hair
greased and streaked
with gold, a violet
nosegay pinned to her
torn evening gown, rubies
rusted under her nose.
A mop of a woman.
I'd wrap my arm
around her
and she would moan
softly, her knees
cracking and eyes rolling.
All night long her small
breath in my hair,
on my ear, kept
me company, listening
to her heart sing,
"Zing! Zing! Zing!"

JUNE MAIL

Love looks like a nightgown gone
to fetch a letter in the daytime.
I can hear your handwriting unraveling
like string as it unfolds in my ear.

The distance between us is as cold as marble,
a conversation between statues. I admire your feet
across the floor, unable to move or walk,
as if it my responsibility to open the lid
of your chest. The heart inside is a heavy pendulum
and still I can see the faint shadow of my name.

I am no more the lover you had
when you left, distilling your body from mine
as you recede into the stationary. In the head
of an evaporating cloud I can see your dull innards,
a transparent blueprint covered in the signature
of my fingertips. I wonder if it is my own reflection.

Once I read your breath, divined as a tea leaf
in my cupped hand, its flat landscape
already turned to moss blooms. The foul knoll
of your body had been shared and shared again
like a telegram sticky with other men's glue.

You cried once, back arced against the sheets, dull
waves radiating from your naked chest into the covers.
I felt the correspondence, a tin note sparking
inside you, my hand a gentle psychic, rereading
your body as it revises itself against me,
rises into others.

PORNOGRAPHY

We all know the difficulty of pants
sliding down over the tops of one's shoes,
yet I am all kerosene and glowing
at task: unpeeling myself at your knees,
pretending not to notice on your face
the ruddy thrill that blooms before contact.

The angle of our stare without contact
is teased by meeting not your eyes but pants,
a supplement to better light your face.
I want to look but nobly face your shoes
with one hand on your chapped and trembling knee.
The other, like a bridle, is glowing.

Pretend the monitor isn't glowing
and you and I will both soon make contact,
straining to look at your eyes, not your knees
and happy just to stroke your endless pants,
tossing the dead animals of your shoes,
moving in to kiss your red, silent face.

By heart, I know the look upon your face
even though I'm audience (and glowing)
that aches to undress you, unlace your shoes:
the absence of our touch is still contact
even before the removing of pants,
the flint of what's to happen in our knees.

Think about the part when I see your knees
connected to the flesh that meets your face,
the secret to be learned about your pants
is realizing we share a glowing
identity, fires making contact
in mirrors, both of us still wearing shoes.

And then the moment you'd take off my shoes—
to feel your ghostly hand between my knees...
I have the tender feeling of contact
though through the dark I cannot see your face,
managing without a touch some glowing
without knowing where you will lay your pants.

Toes curling in shoes, you would touch my face,
careless about knees, but tend the glowing
release of contact with or without pants

SOCIOLOGY

You lecture class and I take notes. We stare
at each other a little. Light catches
your silky scalp and golden pubic hair—

or so I imagine. It's on a dare
I give myself, scribbling poems in snatches
while you lecture class. Taking notes, we stare

a second longer now. I will be fair
and say you're polite, but your eye latches
to my fixed gaze. Your golden pubic hair

is suggested by your scalp, giving care
to point my glances here. This detaches
you from the class lecture, your notes. I stare

at your hand in your pocket, fiddling there.
You direct class to change their seats. Flashes
of your scalp, gold daydreams of pubic hair,

freeze me up when choosing the closest chair
to mine and the class pairs into matches.
I'm the odd man out and you turn to stare:
fly unzipped, hints of golden pubic hair.

BAROMETER BODIES

I flicker on and off in arrival
of the fall. Look at how my body's clock
turned into a barometer. I'm tall
among the loose-leaf trees, strolling the block,

listening to my mind flip on and off.
My youngest brother's birthday came the day
before. Into my fist I smoke a cough
and watch a truck my mother's parents pay

to store and pack their extra furniture
in our garage. My brother got too old
to live here at home. Stooped in curvature
my grandparents woke up and we were told

their minds kept turning on and off. I find
all of autumn's a love of rust and rind.

PART

We were on the phone for four hours
by then and you told me to tell you a story
about birds. Small colors of the morning
were coming through the phone and I could
just make out their wings on the receiver.
I said you were my little bird because of the photograph
you'd taken on the roof, bare-footed, lank and wild,
as if your feathers had just faded back
into your body. I could imagine you
falling asleep while my voice grated
against your speaker, the birds and their chorale
sparking against your naked back, and the downy
trefoil of your breath fluffing your pillows
instead of my hands, whom begged to do it.
You were as new and strange to me as the cloudy
rim of sleep is each night. Still, even now,
at the distance that has crawled between us
and the strangeness you have arrived at once again,
I dream of smoothing back the part in your hair.

DAVID KEALI'I

Honest Flame

DAVID KEALI'I is a Native Hawaiian poet who was born and raised in Western Massachusetts. In 2009 he represented the city of Worcester, Massachusetts, with four other poets at the National Poetry Slam. His work also appears in *'Ōiwi: A Native Hawaiian Journal*, *Yellow Medicine Review*, *Radius*, and *Mauri Ola: Contemporary Polynesian Poetry in English* (Whetu Moana, Volume II). He is a Master's of Library and Information Science candidate at the University of Hawai'i at Mānoa.

HISTORY

The Goddess Hiʻiaka traveled with her
female companion Wahineʻomaʻo,
who expressed her desire for the goddess.
This was not erased through centuries of retelling
was not erased even after Christianity and translation.

Further down lies the memory
of the High Chief Liloa embraced
by his male lover,
the imprint of lauhala mats
deep in their skin.

More recently, Kamehameha the Third
forced to cast aside his lover Kaomi
in favor of missionary influence.

We are still here,
We have always been here.

We are in your moʻolelo.
We are in your moʻo kūʻauhau
Now let it speak.

2:23 AM

There should have been raspberry jam
spread thick over well-buttered toast.

There should have been brick buildings
behind which sun set in peacock plumes of
dusty orange that trumpet-stream
seeing Detroit for the first time.

There should have been dreams that belly-buckled
simply because they were slivered love letters
that couldn't escape.

There should have been the waterfalls of Ithaca
forever melded into mosaics with Shiva dancing
before drum beats.

There should have been a green tea infused with a
Tennessee Waltz fragrance caught in a downpour.

Finally, there should have been the rapture of crooning
that first kiss into something it never was:
fireflies, a solo by Miles Davis,
sparks catching honest flame.

PRETENSE

Liam let it fall:

his guard

the cliché beneath his sternum

the pretense that he was always innocent,
didn't like the draw of a possible burn.

His hands empty for the first time in years and he's surprised he doesn't
fidget, doesn't try to rub the green into pennies.

But a knife flash and stubble
thunder crack the back of his mind,
a simple reminder of failed rain and consequences.

How many times must he get tested
before the definition of negative
overtakes his shame.

let it fall

Liam still wonders if he deserves punishment for every confessed lapse in
judgment,
every time he knew better

but ignored the 30 year warnings

or if there is such a thing as resolution,
and if it could possibly
pull him up.

ISLAND MEN
for McKendy Fils-Aime

Brothers,
someone coded diaspora
into our prints.
not that we wanted such
sticky fingers or foreign
dust in our lungs.
our islands seem to
plant us in soil unaccustomed
to the sunlight we need to
better catch distant wind.
it took too long
for me to realize I
sought someone who understood
that potent mixture of
sea water and cane juice.
when I spoke of rice, tropical fruit,
plantations ... I wanted
to know what we shared.
what friendship we could
offer one other.
each time I try to trill my r's
I tripped over the ʻokina
in my middle name.
when reggaeton blasts
from my speakers, I'm
really searching for the connection
to Polynesian drums.
one of us heard French, another
Spanish, Portuguese hovered somewhere,
Hawaiian wasn't that far off
... who whispered creole
or pidgin?
and who mastered
this language we now give
back to the ocean that
birthed us?

WHAT DO GAY GEEKS DREAM OF?

I.

All the troupes and conventions that
slip in between the panels of a comic book.
The naughty things:
    The way light glides off
    the Silver Surfer.
    That flick of Robin's wrist.
    Apollo and the Midnighter
    as the tumble through the
    layers of the multiverse.
    The irony of Jamie Madrox,
    the Multiple Man.

II.

Captain Jack Harkness and Ianto Jones.
No need for slash.

III.

That the X-Men are really
a metaphor for us.

IV.

That we too are present
in the final frontier, Azeroth,
Middle Earth, Gotham City, Eternia,
Metropolis, a Galaxy far far away …
all the places that provide us
with escape.

V.

Messages in L33T
or Binary.
Klingon or Elvish.
Please, speak nerdy
to us.

VI.

Roles.
As in we know the stats
needed to make an excellent
roll playing character.
And, isn't it great to escape
the roll someone else made
for us?

How sweet that toss of
a 20 sided die.

VII.

The person who understands
the word "tap" isn't necessarily
followed by the phrase "that ass."

VIII.

To lie in bed with our favorite superhero
and explain how we too understand masks.
How important they are.
How impotent they make us.

IX.

Expanding the boundaries
of sci-fi and fantasy past
fan-fic, bad movies, and
expendable characters.

X.

Other gay geeks.
Creators such Octaiva Butler,
Chip Delany, Russel T. Davies,
and countless others have proven
we're not alone.

We've never been alone
and this galaxy is only as finite
as our imagination.

FOR R. ORTA AND S. MUBARAK

Memories dart like flies in the house:

His flirtatious grin,
flash of Puerto Rican-green eyes,
the guiding of fingers.

The slide of pants to the floor,
a wrapper tossed away,
the broken smell of latex.
His smooth skin rubbed down
to whispers.

Then the cracked sound
of a belt buckled up,
thick footsteps,
a sliced glance.

He never spoke to me again.

WATCHER

At night, when he gets home from work,
he looks up at the sky and cackles his
bizarre amusement.
In daylight hours he shouts strange
words in a language that sounds nothing
like the myriad of languages that
rickshaw throughout the neighborhood.
Everyone notices how he doesn't
pick the mint despite its heady scent.
Some say he observes the sky
like the old astronomers of Alexandria.
Others ask if on cloudy days
he looks for the dizzy angels who
sheet lighting between pregnant clouds.
Still, people whisper he must see
meteorological patterns as a
kind of divination.
Or a way to commune with God.
His neighbors know nothing.
He is no patient watcher of skies.
His eyes are broken spires, poor
vessels for prayer.
He says the names of
island-flung Gods for protection
or forgiveness.
It makes no difference.
His eyes dart to the sky
because he knows calamity
will soon come to him
just as it did when he
shared his first night sky
with you.

LEGACIES

i.

No one asks the cataloged if they want new names
or new classification systems
attached to their bodies, thoughts, or homes.

The lucky ones have kept their names
while others fight for the right to use
a language that gave the places they call home
a meaning.

ii.

In the old days Gods sprang
from mountains, waters, animals…
the world around.
For 200 years now religion
comes from afar: first boats
now planes.

How strange the God that doesn't
speak your language.

iii.

In some islands at least three
genders were recognized
and each group had a place
within society.
Mahu, Fa'afafine, Takatāpui …
Native words without sin or venom.

Someone must have heard wrong,
looked in the incorrect black book, and mistranslated
these words as "freak" or "abomination."

iv.

Then came the bombs.
Blasts to rearrange atoms,
boil seas that never knew such heat.
Blasts seen for miles carved an ocean's

worth of fire from the water its self.
Such far away islands decimated so
big countries could claim arsenal security.

v.

What name for the sickness unleashed from all those tests?
What do the words "refugee" or "radiation poisoning" sound like
in ʻŌlelo Hawaiʻi, Reo Maʻohi, Rongelap, Marshallese?
Words for leprosy, smallpox, and influenza
had barely accumulated a hundred years worth of scared lips.
How does the word disease sound in your own throat?

vi.

Nothing remains bleak forever.
Ink has remained alive.
Before writing, symbols and patterns
made with needle, chisel, and ink
made sweet dialogue with the stories.
Songs.
Chants.

These letters are new.
The conversation with them
is all too familiar.

What is writing but
tattooed paper?

vii.

We are Caliban's cousins.
Our profit from knowing your words
is we know how to write
back: *indigenize,*
claim this language
as our own.

DEAN KOSTOS

BAOBAB NERVES

DEAN KOSTOS' books include *Rivering*, *Last Supper of the Senses*, *The Sentence That Ends with a Comma*, and *Celestial Rust*. He edited *Pomegranate Seeds: An Anthology of Greek-American Poems* and co-edited *Mama's Boy: Gay Men Write About Their Mothers*. His poems have appeared in *Boulevard*, *Chelsea*, *Cincinnati Review*, *Southwest Review*, *Western Humanities Review*, and on Oprah Winfrey's website *Oxygen.com*. He has taught at the Gallatin School of New York University and Wesleyan; he currently teaches at The City University of New York.

www.deankostos.com

MOMIX
The Joyce Dance Theater, New York

Torsos turn into faces, snarl
into horizons. While mountains emerge
from scrim-chasms, flashing
strobe lights transform spandex

into horizons. While mountains emerge,
voices chant from the pit
& blacklights deform spandex
beasts. Their claws hook

voices, ranting from the pit.
They braid & bellow with syncopated
beats. Their awe unhooks
moments exploding above the audience.

Braiding & bellowing with syncopated
cellos & drums,
moments explode before the audience!
As the dancers dissolve into waves,

cellos & drums
flash from chasm-scrims.
As dancers dissolve into waves,
their torsos turn into faces, snarling.

BLUE GLOW—LAW & ORDER: SVU

First, learn to say "vic" and "perp" as you shuffle toward
another crime scene: a street
filled with dumpsters and cross-dressing hookers. Graffiti
advertises gangs like products. A monosyllabic swagger
proves detectives Benson and Stabler fearless. Wound
tight, they reveal no theory about the man's "slaughter."

But they're still not sure if it was murder or manslaughter.
Back at headquarters, the detectives lean toward
the glass wall where they affix a forensic collage: wound
with tape and photos of the corpse and street.
As neon leaks from the snapshots, Fin swaggers
to his desk and reads a misspelled letter scribbled in graphite.

From the perp? Benson and Stabler graffiti
the glass wall: arrows, circles, underlines. Manslaughter
(or worse?) hovers like a corpse's portrait by Duchamp. Swaggering
into the office, the DA is peeved. He rifles through untoward
photos, unable to find the one taken on Little West 12th Street.
The forensic pathologist bursts into the room, "The wound

wasn't the cause of death. The vic was mummified alive, wound
with gauze . . . suffocated!" A handwriting specialist claims graffiti
is a signature—no two alike. The street
must contain the clues. So far, the perp of the man's slaughter
eludes capture. As the janitor's broom scuffles toward
their desks, Benson, Stabler, and Fin finally stagger

home. A text-message: *Meet me at the abandoned brownstone.* Staggering,
Stabler pries the door: no lights. Biblical scripture wound
like webs: *Thou shalt, thou shalt . . .* Two words
never seemed so ominous. Illegible graffiti
is carved into a banister like a tattoo on a slaughtered
man's arm. What did this Wall Street

broker get himself into? As Benson proceeds, she finds a dead street-
walker stuffed in a refrigerator. Stunned, she staggers
back, stumbling on an altar of candles, wax bleeding. Not manslaughter—
homicide. Even though they've found the vic's wounds,
there are no blood stains. But each crime announces itself like graffiti.
Questions of who and where shuttle toward

Manhattan streets, wound like phrenic nerves. Following
the graffiti, Stabler staggers into the kitchen and sprays Luminol.
The blue glow enlivens blood's trace, the human stain: man's laughter.

LUMINOUS BARGE
   for Michael Hébert

"*Aybair*, not *Heebert*—it's French," he said.
In Julius' Bar and one week less than legal, I fed

on men's attentions. Michael and I clung
to each other, buoyed through smoke that stung

my eyes. "You don't have to go back to Philly—your choice.
Stay in New York, *chez moi*," he said, voicing

to my desire. "I live above the Jackson Hole. Be my guest
if you like burgers—they've got the biggest

and the best. Then we can go upstairs for dessert,"
he added, smiling. "Sounds great," I chirped.

We jammed the relished slabs in
our mouths, grease trickling down our chins.

Upstairs, he muttered, as if in response,
"About this bunk bed—had a roommate once . . ."

Sidestepping the past, he set
records on the turntable, hoping I'd forget,

then swooped back, his arms a cape
around me. The music, the books—the very landscape

of his apartment formed details of a world
that belonged to others. Compelled

to be of it, to drink its air,
I made mental sketches: bureau, Levalors, worn leather

chair. "Is that where you do your reading?"
I asked, padding across the room, proceeding

to look through slippery magazines on the table.
"You edit all these? I asked. "Boy, you're full

of questions," he said. "No, but they're all Conde Nast,
our parent company." I brushed my lips over the contrast

of textures between his cheek and neck—
the smell of soap on skin, of cologne on black

wool. "Listen, my little *kouros*,
some friends are making dinner for us

tomorrow night. I'm sure they'll like you."
I asked, "Are they translators, too?"

"Some, but most have their hands
full with the politics of publishing. And

now, I've got *my* hands full . . ." He leaned
and kissed my closed eyes. "Closer, Dean . . .

Sexual release tendered sleep: I floated
on his bed, a luminous barge, devoted

to him. Suddenly: *Goldfinger!* Shirley Bassey's shrill
voice scraped away sleep like a wooden strigil.

"4:30 AM! What the hell?"
I yelped. Startled, I jolted & fell

out of bed. "Oh, it's that drag queen bartender upstairs,
getting home from work. Just wait, there's

more—Doris Day: *Once I had a secret love*
that lived within the heart of

me. All too soon my secret love . . .
shuddered through the floorboards, loud enough

for each word to arrive intact. "Don't worry," Michael
comforted, "he'll finish his drunken cycle

and the music will eventually end."
Michael eventually moved to California. I wended

my life to New York. Passing the Jackson Hole on East 64th,
I've been tempted to ring his buzzer. In truth,

I know he's not there, but I imagine the buzzer will activate
a memory-machine bringing back expatriated

selves—promises long erased.
A dusty July. Friends and I subway Manhattan's maze

to the Great Lawn, to view that multicolored cemetery:
The Quilt. I navigate grave-sized panels—territory

sprawling like patches of farmland seen from sky.
I guess we're lucky beauty can lie,

I think with a stifled laugh,
then glimpse a blue, appliquéd epitaph:

                    Translator of French * Ami Très Cher
                           Michael Hébert

HOMAGE TO ALAN TURING

> At the University of Cambridge, the young mathematician
> Alan Turing conceived the fundamental principle of the
> modern computer. This concept did not become a reality
> until after Turing's contribution to the Allied victory in
> World War II, when he broke the Nazis' Enigma code.

Because God would be a Mathematician, computing trees
to branch, leaves to uncurl,
ferns to unfurl—

Because you saw a pine-cone configure its pangolin-petals
into the meter of Sanskrit
prosody—

Because the Fibonacci Series spiraled, arcs connecting
corners, swooping into characters,
a language—

Because arcane ciphers buzzed in a Nazi contraption
(*Satan ex machina*) you pressed your brain
to that malevolent whir—

Because you bent over Enigma at the Government
Code & Cipher School,
defending England—

Because Gödel's Incompleteness Theorem
named an uncaused cause beyond containment,
you magicked an oracle in a box—

Because you endowed the electronic mind
with spinning cryptograms, a vernacular
of brainwork—

Because you created "Colossus" to decipher codes,
win a chess game, expound a theology
of hissing stars—

Because you watched *Snow White & the Seven Dwarfs*,
a prince emerged, silvered
in an all-seeing mirror—

Because you were sex as well as cortex, your eyes
fell on a young man who materialized
out of Manchester's fog—

Because his tousled hair and immaculate flesh
solidified out of rain and desire,
an elemental sacrament—

Because you loved a man, you were deemed criminal.
Even as Europe pardoned Nazis, you faced sentencing:
prison or chemical castration—

Because you chose the latter, your manhood and its desires
retracted. You grew breasts
beneath your tweed vest—

Because you sank into darkness, tumbling from England
and the world, your voice crumbled
into inaudible ciphers—

Because you injected Eve's fruit with cyanide
and bit into its skin, you were ensorcelled
in a swoon, dissolving

into a blank screen, a matrix of transistors,
phosphor throbbing with the world's
intelligence—

Because the Apple logo now bleeds with your poisoned
saliva, your mouth crusted with decades
of silence—

Because I can love another man, and because this world
all too willingly forgets, I thank you, writing this
on a computer.

MISS HAVISHAM

Lace. I will hoard it, color
of tarnished mirrors and mold.
Lace tatted by eyelash-
legs of spiders. And now
lace conceals everything—
windows, rancid wedding cake,
my eyes.

But instead of webs
weaving a curtain—a scrim
obscuring sight—they filter all
I see: I now know what will
never cross the wizened
threshold of self.
No one

will suckle my arid breasts,
no man, no infant.
Below the window, urchins
spit my name, "Hag!"
From the ivory satin flounces
of my gown, from the sugared tiers,
I scrape

rat droppings with my nails.
The cake-top figurines
have long since collapsed
into rotten avalanches,
wedges of icing—mortar
sealing a house, a room,
a life.

Dean Kostos

AMADOU DIALLO'S GHOST REMINISCES

> *An unarmed West African immigrant with no criminal record was killed on February 4, 1999 by four New York City police officers who fired 41 shots at him in the doorway of his Bronx apartment building.*
> — The New York Times

Ice cream tasted like America.
I bought a pint that night, caramel flecked
with almonds.   Celebration!
Sold more than my quota of gloves, scarves

& key chains. Saving for college. Savoring
spoonfuls, I ambled back to Wheeler Avenue,
back to the vestibule—
a bulb the only light,

bald eye.   Voices
pounced from darkness:
"Police—hold it. Stay there."
But they wore jackets & jeans. I fumbled

with keys, couldn't—
"Turn around. Keep your hands
where we can see them," they snarled.
Shouts from every angle—

a hive of voices.
I couldn't think, couldn't act
fast enough—dropped
my keys, the ice cream.

"Here—my hands!"   I thrust them up
to the crescent moon,
my palms' pages waiting
to be inscribed.

"Yeah, that's him! Kid, show us I.D."
As I jammed hand into pocket
to grab my wallet, I looked
down, saw ice cream oozing from crushed cardboard.

"Gun—he's got a gun!" a cop growled.
Their voices became one

voice, their mouths the muzzles
of guns.				Metallic words bit

into me—one after one—
gashes—one after one—leaden flies
swarming, tearing my flesh.
What had I done? I tried

to ask, but fell . . .			couldn't fall far
enough, couldn't be slaughtered fast
enough, sharp metal
pumping into me, blood

sluicing pavement cracks,
the slivered moon reflected
in crimson. Bullets drilled
until I closed my lids:

saw myself float toward the vestibule, saw
myself slip through its closed door,
my forty-one eyes
gleaming.

LIBERATION

> *You're no real pagan, but the kind of pagan who runs alongside our Christian religion.*
> — Carl Jung, The Red Book; after plate #119

This jungle is endless lizard: emerald
plates glister into leaves.
Eyes.

A tail-liana tangles. A knight
in blue-white robe
scales

green scales, wielding a cutlass.
Up, up the aquiline
profile of cliff

he inches. But the branches
snap back on this
homunculus,

trapped in circularity, a question answered
by a spiral.
Hacked

lizard-limbs tumble over ropy strands.
Coral-red roots.
Baobab nerves.

The man tries to free himself
from a chaos of talons.
Why can't he simply flee

this green labyrinth, this architected
God-coil—luring, ensnaring—
keeping him

from the gold-leafed background,
where an invisible icon throbs,
throbs?

CHRYSANTHEMUM
    Based on Carl Jung's The Red Book, plate #169

Sun—aquatic chrysanthemum—
spawns larvae.

Blue heads bubble from an ocean
of *Akasha**—primordial

developing tank.
Silver salts entice

ghostly faces from latency:
Freud, van Gogh,

Suor Juana, Sappho,
Michelangelo, Keller,

Hitler.
They breathe

heft & flesh, evolve,
revolve, until fading

into shades, receding
into ether—fifth substance—

where all flesh liquefies,
where death blossoms

in the script & scripture
of bone.

---

*The Sanskrit word *Akasha* means ether. In its adjectival form, it refers to the "Akashic records," an ethereal compendium of all knowledge and history.

ANTHONY LIOI

DEAR TYLER

ANTHONY LIOI is a denizen of the swamps of New Jersey and a lost citizen of Providence, Rhode Island. His poetry has appeared in *Watershed*, *Environmental Philosophy*, *EarthFirst! Journal*, *Blast Furnace*, *The Dark Mountain Project*, *Borderline*, and *Numinous*. He teaches writing, American literature, and the environmental humanities at the Juilliard School in New York.

Anthony Lioi

A SPELL FOR TYLER CLEMENTI,

who jumped off the George Washington Bridge after his college roommate caught him on camera being gay

Listen, kid, I get it: I went to Rutgers too,
I'm from Jersey, and we each remember
Smear the Queer and all the other torture
games that made us get the hell out of
Dodge, or Mt. Laurel, hoping that college
would dispatch the barbarian hordes at
the mall, the pep rallies, gym class.

I am, as they say, sympathetic. After all,
you could be my blood, my nephew, my
neighbor. And there's more of you where
you came from, contemplating release
that would come from jumping, or wrist-
cutting, or running a car into a tree after
an all-night bender, really just an accident.

The wonders of the Internet didn't do you
in, the methods and motivation fell out
in a climate of hot fear that stank up your
dorm room like stale sweat socks, like puke
in the hallway after a kegger. Hot fear
you brought from home in the minivan,
the loss of refuge, family, honor, the hope

of love. See, I know you, who came to me
saying that Jesus Hates Fags and you're a
believer, how your parents would disown
you, and that's why it took you so long to
call the hotline, talk to a teacher, enter the
infamous SEXPOWERGOD dance party
so shy, without even a lousy drink in hand.

But you never got that far; close enough for
noise, not signal. That's the part I don't get:
you'd made it out of high school, across the
invisible finish line to technical adulthood,
but still in thirteenth grade, not quite out of
the woods, wanting to go it alone, maybe
like that kid who died in Alaska trying to be

Anthony Lioi

Thoreau, Alexander Supertramp. Yes, Bowie
knows it's hard to be a space oddity, but
Planet Earth is blue and there's something we
can do. Sweet ghost, dear Tyler, it's time to gather
up the bits of you spread out across the Web:
the pose of Clementi-playing-violin, the grief
of your parents, the roommate's mug shots, time

to focus hard from your new vantage point as
earth. The children close to jump, crash, cut,
each the intimate of fear, help them track
this viral meme, the signal raining from the
frogs, clouds, Bach, the filthy Raritan, every iPod
and street sign, Manhattan, Bangalore, and
absolutely all the stars in September's sky, see

them recognize that sovereign cry when everything says:

Don't go.

TO THE BOYS KISSING ON THE T,

The tunnels of Boston are not a likely
scene of love. The ooze is only ooze;
after rain, floods erupt in dank holes
unlike the dank holes of our friends.
No arcadia here, whatever the kids
at MIT have told us. The train
plunges into light; after a breath,
you lean one into other. I think,
Those boys are going to kiss on the T!
The river wavers under us, and then
you achieve conspiracy, a master plan,
grand theft and a stunning special effect.
Trains tilt: commuters avert eyes,
sails tack away, but your fusion
seizes them, compels each element
to circumscribe your binary star.
Solar systems evolve; genes barter—
we can hope for intelligent life after
a period of ardor. Which is to say:
Much obliged. It isn't every day that
Boston breaks into bliss just because
two boys are kissing on the T.

Anthony Lioi

THE SHARK AT FOX POINT
after Frank O'Hara

The window on Wickenden is empty.
George and Irene's window is empty.
The window at Aqualife Fish is empty.
The window in Providence is empty.

At first the tank promised perfect water.
The 200 gallon tank promised perfect water
and a dogfish shark of the family *Squalidae*.
That shark stalked the currents of Providence.

The dogfish was the delight of the people.
The shark swam in the mighty ocean tank
that Rhode Island fishkeeping might reign!
That shark was a wonder of Providence.

Then, à la Marilyn Monroe, the dogfish died.
The tank had been drained only minutes from the sea.
Like Robert Kennedy, the shark was murdered.
The shark was martyred only minutes from the sea.

The mighty tank lies empty only minutes from the sea,
but George and Irene go to work in the window because
like Elvis and Jesus and the Pawtucket Red Sox
that shark is resurrection, that shark is the light of love,

That shark is the wonder of Providence!

THE PRINCESS OF PARAMUS WEDS THE KING OF CONNECTICUT
for Jason and Kauser

Whether bronze of dress or folds of samurai ring,
the light finds you each moment, shining at yourselves
and even to us in this momentary paradise. Eclipsing
the Monterey sun and the plunge to ocean at Big Sur,
this radiance surpasses the rock-whale, the sea rose,
the history of Spanish empire, and the sudden betrayal

of hairdresser, not to be mentioned again on earth.
We dance: the music of Providence soars as it ends,
reveals an unsuspected destiny in a sister-in-law's
I told you so. For this reason the rain's archangels
relent, recognize a blessèd element in the world's
harmonium. What was it that made you afraid?

That you would never find a worthy love?
Never kiss in a garden in sight of the sea?

AFTER THE ROMAN PIETÀ
for Siamo Cinque

Bullet-proof glass assures—no one
will take a chunk of him again. Safe
sequestered, the man, beautiful in death,
reclines against his younger mother, standing
for the sky, the earth, all creatures who endure
against the end of what they love. Her eyes
are for him, on him, and yet everyone
lost to war, plague, and the slow drip
of the eon's poisons will also know mercy
in that gaze. It—I mean mercy, and the
bullet-proof glass—assures us: three days late
we will rise in the embrace of earth and sky,
our lives fleshed in a soft rock, suggesting
the flow of water from a fountain without end.

WHAT TO SAY NEXT

If you sit at the rocks under December blue
on the Jersey shore, south of Atlantic City,
the sanderlings tell you what to say next.

The ferris wheel floats in Arcadian iron
drawing emptiness to ward against calamity.
If you sit at the rocks under December blue,

concrete columns heft the Music Hall in air,
shelter a boy, a father after the jetty.
The sanderlings tell you what to say next.

Five white stones, two scallops pocketed,
a whelk hurled back will number a sea
if you sit at the rocks under December blue.

Prima's pizza mutes the danger of snow
for a board-walk: rosemary scents the sky,
the sanderlings tell you what to say next.

Scuttled after the moon's water, we are
suffered to witness as birds invent the *I*:
if you sit at the rocks under December blue
the sanderlings tell you what to say next.

Anthony Lioi

SESTINA FOR HIGH FRUCTOSE CORN SYRUP

Sing high fructose corn syrup,
joy juice of juvenile diabetes!
Politics isn't all metabolism
unless you're a sugardaddy
adumbrated by agribusiness
to destroy the children of America.

In the hospital we call America
an intravenous drip of corn syrup
is provided to patients by agribusiness;
if it happens to sponsor diabetes
so be it, if you're a sugar, daddy,
spreading an agony of metabolism.

Could there be a sweeter metabolism
for the pure products of America?
If we liquified the common sugardaddy
as an ingredient for corn syrup
there would be fewer cases of diabetes
and a run on jobs in the business.

Maybe the secret of this business
is a coup in the national metabolism,
an executive and congressional diabetes
powered by the pop-tarts of America,
a regime of high fructose corn syrup,
the aegis of President Sugardaddy.

Yes! When I say sugardaddy
I mean an overlord of agribusiness
whose stones churn out syrup,
key ingredient in a metabolism
that includes everyone in America
though his favorite is still diabetes.

Anthony Lioi

The real honey of diabetes
has nothing to do with a sugardaddy:
the Food Führer of America
is only a bon bon for agribusiness
as it infects the planet's metabolism
with the virus of corn syrup.

America's an empire of diabetes,
corn syrup the daddy of sugars,
But the fall of metabolism—that's a lordly business.

Anthony Lioi

AN ALLEGORY OF LIFE AT THE MENLO PARK MALL
for Jack Paxton

As the Angles, ancient Klingons,
tell it, life is a bird flying
through the mead hall—from where,
no one knows—over the roof-
beams in drunken glory and out—
where, not even Saxons know.

Here at the Menlo Park Mall
(in Edison, New Jersey)
the Genuine Newark Italian
Hot Dog stand, Route 1 North,
waves its green white & red
after endless years in La Merica.

Jack the Medigan sits outside
Eddie Bauer eating chocolate chip
cookies with a Mocha Latté from
—where else?—Starbucks. Tall
and strong enough to be Klingon,
Jack's from West Orange, Earth,

so an Italian Hot Dog joint
appears genuine to sensors.
We concur that Italian Sector is
Odyssean: cyclopses in cheap
Hawaiian shirts, siren daughters,
and Poseidon right on your tail.

Out of spandrels that make
this mall a mosque to Mammon,
an iridescent meteor, a satellite
falls—a bird—a starling, invader
and not to be mourned according to
the Church of Christ, Darwinist.

It lights at the display featuring
men's seersucker shirts. Then it
flies past the Nature Store towards
Nordstrom. We conclude that life
is a bird, but how it got malled,
how in the name of *Trek* it escapes,

no one knows.

Anthony Lioi

TRILOBITE

n. Any of the numerous extinct marine arthropods of the class *Trilobita*, of the Paleozoic era, having a segmented exoskeleton divided by grooves or furrows into three longitudinal lobes.

— The American Heritage Dictionary

You had no cell phones—
the sea was sweet without
satellite communication or
the latest coffeehouse in Prague.
In fact, given fossil photographs—
shovel-headed centipedish spider-mite—
you make the horseshoe crab
who lately spawned at Brigantine
appear the sleek Manhattanite.

If, as I recall, you perished at the Permian frontier,
could you clear something up: what's death-by-asteroid
feel like? My species is conducting little tests.
No asteroids—we're not Zeus yet,
but cowfart, Oldsmobiles, and the mysteries of Wal-Mart
pull a whack-job on the kingdoms of the living.
Anyway, annihilation:
Does it hurt?
Is it a hoot?
Do extinction-angels giggle as the last of you bite it?
Is it being sealed in glass,
Sleeping Beauty with no prince to kiss 'er?
Or driving Jersey's Turnpike when everyone has EZ-Pass
and you've got a quarter.

Maybe you should save your breath.
Just answer this:
Did you pardon the bullet that ended your age,
or sit at eternity's HDTV
longing for mammals to die in a blur
of scorched milk and burnt fur?

THE DESERT, SIGNS AND WONDERS

The O'odham say *the desert smells like rain*—
survival is more than the end of extinction—
cactus blossoms rise from the waves of dust.

In Agua Prieta, gardens crack the streets,
a permanent culture of water's victory.
The O'odham say the desert smells like rain.

The quail and her children wrangle Tucson,
Coyote flips McMansions on a dare,
cactus blossoms rise from the waves of dust.

Saguaros shunt the storm of the sun
to ruby fruit for human, bat, and bee.
The O'odham say the desert smells like rain.

Hummingbirds flood the willows,
ironwood weathers like suburbs and stone,
cactus blossoms rise from the waves of dust.

This one never calls the desert dead:
it's a dry kind of heat in a feverish world.
The O'odham say the desert smells like rain;
cactus blossoms rise from the waves of dust.

Anthony Lioi

IN PRAISE OF DAISY THE DACHSHUND

The difference of her sitting and standing is
    slight enough
to illuminate the coincidence of opposites.

In barking at invisible Intelligence,
    she teaches
discernment of spirits and the majesty of signs.

Among high shanks, she monitors her far domains,
    surveying
a window of paws, teeth, and tongue.

Lost in lap, sustaining the sweetest petting,
    she opines
that the world may not be an error, after all.

Coming to rest, a dachshund indulges the
    eldest urges
to assert the dignity and eminence of dog.

PHILIP MATTHEWS

LETTERS FROM THE LOWLANDS

PHILIP MATTHEWS is a gallery assistant at The Pulitzer Foundation for the Arts in St. Louis. He is also a Jr. Writer-in-Residence at Washington University in St. Louis where he teaches poetry and creative nonfiction. His work has recently appeared or is forthcoming in *Sonora Review*, *The Tusculum Review*, *Zone 3*, *The Puritan*, and *Super Arrow*, among other journals.

www.twitter.com/philiplm26

[HANDS GREW OVER MY HIPS]

—Hands grew over my hips.
Tell me
when you're close, you said.
I asked, *Close to what.*
You laughed. I watched
your fish press
lips in its bowl: silver
globes rising into
rings, caught at the surface.
You think he knows
he's in there, I might have
asked, because you answered
There and I came.
The fish zipped up,
reclaimed a pocket of air.
Superman, Invisible Woman:
plastic eyes jellied.

[LIGHT THROUGH THE BROKEN SHUTTERS]

Light through the broken shutters
dusts the room. Men cover me
with fingernails: my polished face.

Pulling out the wires, it feels good
not to stay quiet:
fish come hissing from our throats.

*

Carver, you can make me

a pretty boy or happy / crime against skin

The neighbors come raising fire
Trim my lips they cannot bear in oiled boats

Cover me up in sawdust, what you like

I'll be a bird sleeping

I'll glow

[REMEMBER WHEN GRANDMOTHER WALKED IN ON US]

Remember when Grandmother walked in on us,
saplings snapping apart
in the gale that is Grace Slick.
She seized: *She tried to poison the president!*
Debris.

A monster woke under my skin
for years I didn't sleep, considering Grace.
How treason is made into sex.
How a bomb thanks the establishment for its existence.

*

Sunday we took to the streets,
bracing arms, snapping ass.
The river threw up. The guards rushed in,
filled their skewers with us.
Picture hogs.

You taught me how to survive:
I let somebody in charge fuck me.

[XXX-XX-5262: CONTAMINATED]

xxx-xx-5262: contaminated

Ink blots the cock-drilled ego
in the Petri dish

Happy Flag Day, spoiled boy
Throw up your hands to the microscope

The rot forms lungs around land

We know what for

*

Friday, March 13. The FGAT has ordered the immediate override of genetic systems deemed *corrupt and intolerable* under 6696. I've been subpoenaed for neurological upload of the Alpha Male Mutation. —Even in her weakest years, when Grandmother thought to die, she couldn't.

[TONIGHT]

Tonight,
the Mardi Gras Indians flocked
the streets, sang *See my king*
out of the pot-holes,
until a child, apple-rot
on his father's shoulders
setting a camera,
called *Over here, faggots!*
and one of them turned,
charged into his light:

A flash thru flesh:

A chameleon whipped into grit:

His claws in the boy's leg,
meaning *keep*.

[DON'T BE A BABY. DON'T SULK]

Don't be a baby. Don't sulk
at the drunk-up bottle because you're thirsty
for the comfort of *there*. There
are no more lifejackets. Did you know
orcas toss otters around live before they eat them?
No one knows why. I don't suppose they can
confirm themselves. Can you?
Maybe it's to teach their calves *prey*,
or maybe they're just playing sadist. I used to
rub mine red in the backseat
when Dad filled up his gas tank. I liked
the fumes. Learn to swim.

[VALID RELATIONSHIPS ARE CONISTENT]*

Valid relationships are consistent. For example, mines are placed in the water: even practiced submarines touch them. According to the broadcasted psychologist, the stigma against same-sex couples relates to their social behavior, which is others' regular perception of a core thing about who they are. Kids illegally. Radically anti-human. A man and a man a distortion of the ideal married father marriage, that responsible touchstone the whole family can touch. The hands are placed, mine, mine, their official capacity. Plaintiffs are two same-sex couples. Plaintiffs contend that their freedom to marry is a fundamental right protected by the Due Process Clause. It is not. Plaintiffs constitute an irrelevant class. The majority define the basis of sexual orientation, which is psychology, which can be changed. The Alpha Male Mutation neurological attachment can rewire any sick system. It worms through the synapses, communicating government to citizen, family to island, hierarchical as god intended. A multitude of heterosexual-positive television, radio and internet-based advertisements and messages transmitted in seconds. Side effects may include headache, facial flushing, upset stomach, less commonly, bluish vision, blurred vision, sensitivity to light. In rare instances, men reported a sudden loss of vision. It is not possible to determine whether these events are related directly to the Alpha Male Mutation treatment or to other factors. If you experience compromise or loss, we are not liable. You are not based on objective data or discernible methodology. Assigning individuals to care for you is heavy for the state—the supreme rig.

---

* "[Valid relationships are consistent]" incorporates some erasure of the ruling written by Judge Vaughn R. Walker—of the United States District Court for the Northern District of California—which overturned Proposition 8. The "side effects" in this section are appropriated from viagra.com.

[I SLEEP IN]

I sleep in.
The city can keep its topless girls

who name the roaches in their shotguns.
The pets scuttle over the sink,

cross-stitching legs
after a bread pellet. They sew up.

You show up in my dreams:
we chase the sun down the levee,

or follow a row of men-of-war,
stars pinned in their washed-up bodies.

Always the sky a government,
a kind of dress put on us.

The mind can't prohibit it.

[YOU'RE A PART OF US, FLEE-ER]

You're a part of us, flee-er.

We say to the ax
which grace, over you, suspends,

Come closer.

    [Spilling hands,
    the tar-men hold me down.

    The audience applaud

    my rotting-face,
    lips popped like greased kernels.

    Tongues trespass my mouth—

meet me in a meat shop window, win]

Quiet, animal.

IAN JAMES MORGAN

A LITTLE RESPECT

IAN JAMES MORGAN lives in Cheltenham, UK, and is a graduate of the Creative Writing BA programme at the University of Gloucestershire. He has had poems included in *Desire & Madness* (Boho Press: 2006) and poetry and prose published in the anthology *Under Surveillance* (Boho Press: 2007). Ian explores the dynamics of sexuality, power and addiction. He has been described, sometimes by others, as 'fabulous.'

ROBERT, AGED 11

I'm going to be beautiful;
just like them. I will be Lynda
Carter, Carolyn Jones, Catherine
Bach and Lee Merriweather.

I watch them on TV and copy
their walk, their hair swish,
and wear their own matinee
smile as I stare at my reflection.

But I have short hair and I'm fat
and I live in Swindon.
I don't have bracelets, tight
black outfits or a yellow coupe.

In my mother's full-length
mirror I transform myself
into a modern Aphrodite;
(I'd settle for Joan Collins).

If I try hard enough.
my chubby mounds will bud
into firm breasts; ripe
and succulent. I shall wear

silk dresses, pearls and silver;
drink in bars with friends
at weekends. Men might approach
and buy me wine and roses.

Until then I read books about Diana
Dors, Eartha Kitt and Marilyn;
plan my Saturday depending
on who is on the telly.

For now I tuck my privates
between my legs, try on oversized
heels and make-up my face
before I shower it away.

FASHION MAGAZINE

You are very handsome
and impeccably dressed;
suit trousers pressed

with a sharp crease
to cut wandering hands.
A shirt that contours

gym tortured body
and college coloured tie
to hint at hidden length.

Jacket hung on squared
shoulders; thumb hooked
around belt loop.

But you'd look better still
with my spunk on your face.

DAD DRIVING ME TO SCHOOL

On the radio Erasure sing
a little respect.

You turn it off with a swift
stab of your finger.
Poofters.

The thick silence has an edge;
it separates us.

I hug my Puma bag.
Erasure aren't gay, dad,
only the singer is.

We pass a pelican crossing
and a lollipop lady.
I'm gay. I'm a queer.

Have a good day, son.
One look under my bed
will ruin yours.

DEAR HOUSEMATE

I broke a wine glass
and put pieces
in your make-up bag
and knicker drawer.

I tipped salt
on your freshly
baked scones
and smeared
jism on your pillows.

It wasn't me that spread
rumours about your abortions.
I merely started them.
But I did tell everyone
you fucked a grubby fisherman
on holiday. Then got sick
and shit yourself in bed.

I emptied the freezer
of your frozen chicken pieces.
I tossed it all out in the trash
along with your notes
from the psychology class.

I snapped your cash
card in half.
And yes, I tipped the bleach
on your summer ball dress.

Why?
You want
to know why?

I just don't
fucking
like you.

SERVING THE COUNTRY

My soldier-boy
stands to attention.

He troops the room
in just his boots,
salutes,
and shows off
his weapon.

He treats my ass
to a passing-out
parade: it's all
display and pomp;
then shoots his load
in my new-recruit
mouth; he's a drill
sergeant in spit
and polish.

SMALL TALK

He offers inches
to make me wince;
poses in a chair
with legs spread
to display what
he strokes.

A smirk; so sure
as each movement
pulls me closer,
neither one
of us says a word.

He bites his lower
lip as I go straight
to my knees;
then pats the side
of my head:
good boy.

ORGAN GRINDERS

We'll smoke afterwards. I'll smile
and suggest drinks but they just
wipe off and go. I get vague
commitments to text and I say

*that will be fine; why don't you
bring a friend next time?*
So I lick my fingertips and drink
as I watch 'Notting Hill.'

I fuck for moments when
a man's clammy hands
might fool me into thinking
he more than likes me. Maybe.

They've taught me well—I can suck
with gusto and I know exactly
when to moan, when to arch
as I'm bare-backed or roasted.

Then in the week I'll turn my head
as my phone bleeps and vibrates
on a coffee table: '*Hey, I'm horny;
what are you doing tonight?*'

You. Obviously.

FIGURES

Doctor Stone spends days
in equations, projections
and quantum mathematics.

The evening is his passport:
white and grey are replaced
with gold, green and brown.

Tonight he is Wing-Li
the autumn garden princess;
who asks a man hung

with eleven inches to bury
himself, right up to the hilt,
in her behind.

She pays him three hundred
American dollars then cries
after he leaves.

CREDIT CRUNCH

The foreman announces
that the labourers
aren't needed this afternoon.

So John buys himself
a lunchtime treat;

the massage parlour
isn't far from the site.

He drops his work boots
by the flaking blue door

and pulls down his cement
flecked sweatpants.

She's thorough and swallows,
keen to get repeat business;
'my name's Tiffany.'

His wipes his palms
on his pale hairy thighs,
'I don't care, love.'

STEPHEN POTTER

BOURBON AND GINGER

STEPHEN POTTER, a graduate of Temple University's MA program in Creative Writing: Poetry, lives and works in his native town of Philadelphia. His poems have made scattered, far-flung appearances over the years in magazines such as *ixnay*, *Aufgabe*, *Mirage #4 Period(ical)*, *American Poetry Review*, *EOAGH*, and in *Blood and Tears: Poems for Matthew Shepard*. He is still not sure how he became a marketer in the construction industry—his "accidental career"—but he's working on poems about it.

A POSTCARD TO DIRK YATES

Those ostensibly straight pornos
you shot with gay guys in mind—

I can't tell you how many of my friends
rocked out to them. Only a few

admitted to acquiring a taste for watching
straight guys get off. We were particularly

fond of that stud with the sketchy
8 ball tattoo on his upper arm.

I saw him once in a purely homo
boot camp fantasy & he looked

out-of-place, the one
tentative face in the circle-jerk.

Whatever happened to him?
Please write & let me know

so I can post it on Facebook. Let's
take pity on those too shy to ask.

POSTCARD & POSTSCRIPT TO THE LADY
SITTING BEHIND MICHAEL AT MIXTO RESTAURANT

Clearly the words 'circle' & 'jerk'
used together have a magical ability
to penetrate the enchanted ring of bourgeois
conversation & make heads swivel Linda
Blair-like to target the speaker with a glare
meant to rivet his mouth shut with shame.

I was reading a poem to my friend Michael. You
apparently were minding other people's business.
My apologies if it wasn't inspired by that
other Mary, Poppins, who brought
you & yours to Mixto for pre-show cocktailitos,
some paella, & lengthy comparisons of handheld
devices with clever names. I think yours
needs to be set on 'vibrate,' if not 'stun.'

         Kisses,
           Steve

         P.S. Just for you
my next poem will feature fat, uncut dicks
& a golden shower sequence that out-
dazzles the aquatic acrobatics of even
the best Esther Williams movie
before I reign in my dolphins with a snap!
                  snap!
                          snap!

A POSTCARD FROM LADY GAGA

The pinot grigio has finally warmed
under the sun's lidless gaze and
here I am, dropping another famous
name to delineate those orbits
I cross and keep. My fondest wish
is that through your fascination with
the woman attached to the name,
we'll build a bridge over these Hampton
waters, however faint, and let
some feeling pass between us.
Father Time is growing old
my little monsters, so hurry, hurry
before his magic hour dissolves!
I can't claim to say I wish you were here
but I sincerely hope you do.

A POSTCARD FROM EDDIE RABBITT

I'm surprised I received your card, Eddie,
in light of the fact you're dead. I hope
wherever you are, your lungs are in the pink.
Been thinking about you lately, how
I'd listen to "Someone Could Lose a Heart Tonight"
and sink into myself, thinking *someday I'll know
what this song is all about*, priming the spot
where I'd eventually put the drama in my queen,
some shuffle in my two-step, and a tear on my pillow
when all the conditions were right.

FAR FROM HEAVEN

In the ornate urban park
a husband kneels beneath trees and a trench coat.

It's late. It's after a business dinner
strategizing how to lose his coworkers.

It dissolves in bourbon and ginger
at the pressed-white party.

That his wife arranges the details
to mask the taste of salt

foreshadows the many calls made from rented rooms
where young men lounge on starched beds.

Prolonged silences speak of that grope
toward the right thing to say.

Her words sound like the pale green light
entering her closed window.

Where he goes, she cannot follow,
even in her own way,

so the black gardener returns her lavender scarf
behind the house. On the street

her hand reaches toward the not-possible
where last night her husband slipped

hand out of hand
into the city's nameless bars. He knows

a slow drag on his cigarette is subtler than color.
Her scarf is a flag pulled taut on a twig.

YEAR TO YEAR

As daffodils
        thrust toward
butter, a hunger
        lingers.

Is a wish ever
        slight? The father
said *What is*
        necessary

is never unwise. Not
        the same thing.
Nor do I desire
        returning to

those first thoughts.
        Let's leave
those cherries
        where they lie

in crumpled fields
        forever stained
by practicing
        love. Is it worth

leaving obliquity
        to speak clearly
again? Breathing
        visibly

the father said
        Be my valentine.
I know he wasn't
        talking to me.

DELILAH'S PREMONITION
for Jenna Ogilvie

As they open and close
around your waist
these legs mimic
that device from another time

not yet invented.
What difference
can your hair make now,
your strength

rising up through your pillar
that, once spent, will presage the temple's
heave and collapse: you
crumpled in my arms,

your body shuddering with gratitude
for my razor-sharp technique.

Stephen Potter

GERTRUDE STEIN'S ILLEGIBLE HANDWRITING

Facts like Stein's admission
via Alice B. Toklas in her 'autobiography'
she had illegible handwriting
are important. On page 76 Alice B. writes
I am very often able to read it

when she is not. After sitting for Picasso
issues with legibility
did not hinder Stein's obsessive
investigation of the sentence.
Only recently have I begun to focus on sentences

and my handwriting is coincidentally bad.
In school Sister Assumpta
wrote check marks on my report cards
and without realizing it
I heard 'curse' in 'cursive.'

Most obsess over a different type of sentence—
not a sentence like Rackin's in her old mss.
The Unpredictability of Plant Life with its
syntactic disjunctions and end-
line hinges swinging readers into new tangents,

and not like Jarnot's sentences in *Ring
of Fire*, looping by commas
back to the same
torqued nouns. Stein's influence
is present in both and Stein would say

Commentary is not literature.
Literature is indeed commentary and commentary
can be literature and Rackin
and Jarnot prove this by embedding
private details in surreal landscapes

that flash like music videos
not metaphor. Simile and metaphor
allow the illegible to permeate the eye.
Picasso was a metaphor
but I can't stand his person

despite his accurate portrait of Stein.
Blaine Anderson is not
a metaphor and he
is painting a portrait of me that remixes
lines from my work.

The difficulty here is to talk about
Stein's handwriting
but painting and Picasso
get in the way and I hope Blaine
will straighten this out

because the reader might think I am
comparing myself to Stein.
To read a successful poem
regarding this struggle see Anne Carson's
"Irony is Not Enough:

My Life as Catherine Deneuve."
Note the compression of character, actor, and poet
that navigates the fuzzy realm between fact
and fiction. Friction is also a fact
and this is another type of sentence.

Carson-Deneuve cues this distinction by declaring
This is mental. Associations and pins
are mental but they can also be aural
like H.D.'s sonic footwork
in "Red Rose and a Beggar" where the key vowel

according to Don Riggs
is inserted in the sonic vagina. Personally
I don't know anything about that
but his reading sounds right. A sentence
is a length, a segment. It carries

from A to B; it is sometimes concerned
whether a dog knows it.
Is it six sentences to anyone else in the world?
It seems the most important connection for Picasso
between himself and women

was measured in inches. Rackin and Jarnot
do not delve into such matters.
They are concerned with a different kind of sentence.

Carson noted
the period is a sweater's top button

buttoned up when the lecture ends.
The period is concerned with indicating a duration
between a happening and
a happening is about to occur
but this gap is also a type of event

that cues the reader it's her
pause to breathe. Blaine
doesn't seem concerned with pauses
as he applies layers that erase
then fill in with figures, words,

and warring colors in patches echoing Twombly's
struggle for the heroic in
Fifty Days at Iliam, particularly
the violet red
storm of Achaean rage

ballooning into geometry. The classical inheritance
is tricky to balance. Ironic
considering its focus on balance.
One can argue
Jarnot's poems dance precariously on

the tight wire of climax
as the nouns shift back and forth
adjusting their load of adjectives and verbs.
Stein left nouns to Ezra Pound
and Ezra and others lathed them

into nuts, bolts, cogs, and other
masculine notions rendered objects
and ripe for rescue from that craving for
new poetry movements. The title poem
of Rackin's book exemplifies an organicism

aligned with Stein and
certain feminist practices erupting
like the fractal roots of digital trees.
The last image invokes
illegibility in the realm of the image

although Tory Dent's line about cropped hair
ululating like a cut peony only dogs can hear
comes closer to demonstrating
the creation of images or
sounds that hover beyond the senses.

Certain words of Stein's
after setting them down
dwelled just that side of understanding for her.
They curled up into balls
or lengthened into stringy theories

that defy exactitude. She knew
there were no ideas but in things,
so she wrote a single volume,
divided by three,
in which they came alive.

PATRICK STEVENS

PET SOUNDS

PATRICK STEVENS is an author, poet and scriptwriter from New Jersey. His novel, *The Spins*, is available for download now. His latest collection of poetry, *Rebirth Under Dead Trees*, is forthcoming from unboundCONTENT Press. His poems have appeared in numerous journals including *Breadcrumb Scabs*, *Ascent Aspirations*, *Instigatorzine* and *vox poetica*. Patrick is delighted to have the "Pet Sounds" series included in *Assaracus*. He dedicates these poems to Brian Wilson.

www.thepatrickstevens.com

BOARDS

Well East Coast girls are hip
too slick for knowledge

tight jeans, bikini dancing
in the ignorant offers of fresh air.

Four walls, now that's construction
stud beams sheet rock safety

there is no need for fresh green.
No opacity in the intentions

of the breeze, that heat
could well be Jesus love or hell

so best to seal the shutters
scream four-beat surfer dreams

across the piano keep the pedals
clean, don't let the ephemeral world

leak between your fingers
and the keys and make yourself

a masterpiece you can trust
will never leave.

DAY 167

Day one-hundred-sixty-seven: wake up
smoke two cigarettes in bed
imaginary army clamor in my head
shot shot drill talk orders
"Don't move soldier,
you may do some coke and smirk
but don't complete the Smile."
37 months ago Paul McCartney
blew my mind out in Los Angeles
and everybody felt it
they all saw it then
they turned on me, tried to seize
creative control—like they could know
the proper sweep of a synthesizer
measured blend of English horns

anything at all. They're backup singers
for Christ's sake, so sing
and let me be the genius
let me know better here
upstairs, alone, secure
in my platinum and powder
swimming in old sheets
the stink of this bathrobe
smells like my father
smells like home
these are the trappings of success
that have trapped me off
between four beige corners
four rogue ingrate band members
and forty million dollars' worth of irony

don't move, Brian.
The sergeant may find you.

MOUNT VERNON AND FAIRWAY

It's important to remember
there will be winter everywhere now
or soon a cold snap
even here in sunny California
when the sand dune life dies
a wash of waves crisp
high tides with no riders
crash freeze out the hermit crabs
subside and it is done
even now in summer surf bunnies
shudder at the thought grab a linen shawl
and curl up next to not me

the wife is downstairs tired
of the bed and trying
still she stays industrious
all happy times and sandwiches
and sunshine and infuriating
off to market now for god knows
while genius even now grows
in these pillows and this beard
to be meted out in harmonies
she cannot appreciate through
sips of normal person coffee
no one else is here but they agree

and for that matter Mike
the other day went on a tirade
over "Good Vibrations" said
it was a piece of avant-garde shit
like he knows the score
with his junior high band leader
three notes and three chords
Jesus that simpleton Judas
in my own home-built studio
blasphemy spills from the lips
I made sound beautiful
but forget what he said

it's important to forget
before you attach yourself to sun
the lacy waves of June

nylon strings and lemon yellow
girls who love the old you
it turns cold out there
always no matter what you do
the bold invention of your tune
escapes in colorless dots an ellipsis
on the cool breeze of December
sweeping past the shore and down
the hall reminding you to lock the door.

ODE TO JOY

Beethoven wasn't half deaf at all
he cut the legs from his black piano
to be rid of the voices for once
pressing face to floor to flush them out
in a sweet symphony of drowning

counting out even-metered measure
death in soprano hallelujahs
and the archangels in flugelhorns
being sure to pierce the treason of
his eardrum and the endless whispers

slice their throats away from the anvil
the warmth of their blood inside his skull
dripping from his half-note axe handle
with the murderous victory of
inverted G major harmonies.

I explain this from my one good ear
the reason I still write my music
to one day find the note that slays them
to celebrate with Beethoven the
viscous crimson wet of our freedom.

ON CARNIE, 1971

Carnie is three today or was it yesterday
a sunflower child sent
skyward on a tiny swing

there is no vision
from this window I can only see
that life is cruel

but music must be made
from this orchestral bedroom
the magnum opus still to come

angry voices penning verses
in my head versus children's voices
spinning in the playground

Carnie is my seed but we
lead such disparate lives—
no, she may never know me

but she will grow to see
what daddy runs from; I hide
so my daughter is not haunted.

HEROES AND VILLAINS

Those who claim that music
should be simple should be
hunted and their pianos
smashed for lack of knowledge
lyrics are lesser things boys and girls and charms and love but a melodious
        craft is not for
the two-chord proletariat

it is to be slaved over
composed of feathered angels
yellow poppy opiates
the sudden wings of doves
tucked inside the scientific structure of a parabolic curve and if you are lost
        now then
assume that music composition is not for you

Perhaps I have come across
as haughty when I ought to
have conveyed a different thought
the span between an English
and a French horn is substantial massive really in the wrong hands tin pans
        and tragedy
I weep for that disaster

and how little it must seem to you
but if these songs are to please
our ears and we are little
reflections of Jesus then jesus
why not suffer to perfection? it seems prerequisite any less is blasphemy upon
        the sacred
anvils of the Lord

and yes it is the age
of pressing pop tunes onto vinyl
and not pompous chamber harpsichords
but Mozart Haydn Beethoven
Chopin Debussy Wilson is my polyphonic bloodline and one errant bassoon
        will cheapen
bastardize the efforts of a dynasty

it is tones you see inexplicable
quarter notes and unfilled halves

set in five-line clef-staff increments
which shout aloud my legacy
it is useless to speak their meaning parse through the wretched dictionary for
        vain
translatable phrases and garner nothing but regulatory armistice gumbo
        banana sundresses.

'TIL I DIE

Nothing has come from this wanderlust
combing the beach in midnight blackness

save the sound of my feet cracking shells
crushing their lifeless forms, asserting

Brian Wilson's name to the heavens
so that this afternight existence

does not shrink me down to granular
measure me a jellyfish flopping

formless on the endless Pacific
inscribe on the tides of history

this is all that I was
a cork on the ocean

the spray of the sea
a cork on the ocean.

PETER WELTNER

LION-LIKE

PETER WELTNER has published five books of fiction, including *The Risk of His Music* and *How the Body Prays*, three poetry chapbooks, a collaboration with the artist Galen Garwood, *The One-Winged Body*, and two full-length collections of poems, *News from the World at My Birth: A History* and, most recently, *The Outerlands*. His stories have appeared in several national anthologies, including *Men on Men 4*, *Best Gay American Fiction 3*, and two O. Henry's, in 1993 and 1998. He lives with his partner Atticus Carr, an LCSW, in San Francisco near Ocean Beach.

CONSUBSTANTIATION

1.
In the high northern stained glass window, black-
robed, Luther preaches from his theses rolled
into a scroll. South, facing him, quill dipped
in ink pot, Melancthon writes the Augsburg Confession.
To the east, nearly naked, Jesus hangs on his cross,
his flesh linen white, unstained by noontime sun.
I rise from a regal chair behind the altar,
its flat oak back taller than I am by two feet.
Dressed in cassock, surplice, satin bow, I receive
from Pastor the tray of small communion glasses,
the wine poured from a bottle now also the blood
shed by our Lord. Mindful of his agony,
I don't see beneath my skirt my loose shoe laces.
I trip, fall, spill both, Christ, wine, all.

2.
Mustache cups don chests and window sills.
I'm her heretical pupil, a shy Lutheran boy,
struggling on canvas to copy the image of
Magnus Martyr Sister tore from her order's
calendar. Proud of her sable brush, Senora Ruiz
dips it in her palette's cadmium red, dabs blood
on limbs impaled on spokes of a chaff-cutter wheel.
Pursing her lips, pink as a doll's, she whispers,
That child, Sister, denied the mass's mystery.
Heaven's lost to him, poor soul. Sister hushes her.
Too late. I grab a palette knife, cut an X
across the back of my hand. Taking a stand
for reformation, I paint round my eyes blood
haloes no nun's soap or lye can scrub away.

3.
Wandering the halls of my father's nursing home,
a far gone Lutheran pastor, face tantrum red,
arms wrapped round his body as if bound by
a straightjacket, shuts his eyes to the world,
squeezes blood from tears. Opening them wide,
he shouts, *Amen,* pounds on his chest as if
to make a sacrifice flow from his stricken heart.
Buttons undone, a string holds his p.j.s up.
He shuffles down a wheelchair lined hall

listening to his son, a convert to Rome, expound
on the Shroud of Turin, *the blood soaked in it,*
he says, *our Savior's own.* Pastor's eyes glower.
It's one more Catholic magic trick. Touching pus
on his cheeks, he licks his fingers like candy.

4.
Near closing time, the man scrawls a note on
a napkin, slips it down to me, waits outside
for me to read it, receives beneath the streetlights
the right sign, follows me home up the steep hill.
What if, he says, *that pretty face were splashed
with acid?* He doesn't laugh. It's dark. Music's playing,
a Bach concerto too refined for rough trade,
the game the man's enacting. I pour more pinot.
The taste of it is on his tongue as we kiss. I'm not
afraid. The man says, *Or sliced your skin. What if?,*
our bodies already entwined beyond undoing.
The man bites my lip, teeth sharp enough to make
it bleed. Our mouths taste of blood, wine, wine, blood,
two substances coexisting, one in the other.

FIVE PICTURES WITH SNOW

Coney Island

March by the Atlantic. Along the beach, the waves
reach as high as the snow-covered sand. Phil stands
by my side, dressed for summer in weejuns,
dapper slacks, cotton shirt, spiffy yacht jacket.
His shiny hair stays mysteriously brushed.
His dark eyes stare back at my camera
that looks at him as clearly as a reporter might,
surprised how nobly he won't show he's cold.
When young, a poet, a dancer. Now he's forgotten.
Like a snapshot of a soldier taken before
he's killed, this photo's all I've left of Phil.
Despite the drawer where I store it, the picture
has faded, his face, his clothes, his graceful hands
bleached by the late winter sun's gleaming off snow.

Ice Cap

After it's over, for good, Leif and I turn away
and lie on his sheets, apart, snow starting
to fall from ceiling to floor, unseen by our eyes
but not our hearts, now Arctic cold. We dress
and walk through the park, its moonlit beauty
stark black and white, iron and marble, to a bar
where we stand side by side too scared to move,
as alert as two creatures of the North drifting
from land on the same floe, watchful for men
in boats after their pelts, keen-eyed, aware,
despite the long polar nights, no hunters are
tricked or deceived by their white camouflage,
knowing they're easier to see, to spear, to shoot
as the frost line rises, the ice cap melts.

Peter Weltner

An Obituary in the Alumni Review

Rush week, Bill walks in the Sig house, shaking
snow off his hair, Ham Col's handsomest man.
Too bad he pledges Deke instead. I never talk
to him again, spy him on campus mostly from
a distance, close up once in the gym. That's all.
In his obit, I read he'd married, lost an infant son,
had come out late at thirty-five, lived in Miami,
had a lover, sold party costumes, gardened.
Some memories are never warm, but shiver
like trees that, undressed of their leaves,
are always cold, thoughts of the past icy
as winter winds and storms on College Hill.
It's years too late to know what I know now,
Bill, too late to brush the chill from your hair.

Antarctica

In the Tahoe cabin we'd rented, Kenny leans
on a window frame. His fingernails scratch
ice off a pane. Snow's been falling for more
than a week. Despite two fires blazing inside,
he never quits shivering. He's wasting away.
No one knows why. It's nineteen eighty-one.
Time is cold, Ken says. He tells me a story about
a soldier in Antarctica, swearing it was true.
Out restlessly exploring late one morning,
he wandered too far from the compound. Lost,
squinting despite his goggles, he saw, way off,
identically clothed, his pale twin, a man not
a ghost beckoning him to follow. As he did,
almost frozen when found, babbling, snow blinded.

The Monks of Tibhirine

A man's end is never nothing. It is a snowy day,
cold even for the clothes they're wearing, sweater,
heavy coat, wool scarf, knit cap, the wind too stinging
to look straight into, what's ahead too certain,
their steps halting, unsure, their tracks swiftly
hidden by fast falling flakes, thick as leaves,
hiding all traces of where they've been.   Behind,
beds, a night's sleep, matins to look forward to.
At the end of Beauvois's *Des hommes et des dieux*,
terrorists are leading seven monks from Tibhirine
to be murdered. The winter trek's hard. As they enter
deep woods, all the men—assassins, martyrs—
slowly vanish into the snow. Whiteout. On the screen,
nothing's visible. *All that is is light.*

Peter Weltner

BASTILLE DAY AT THE CAPRI

The Capri's partying on the night of Bastille Day.
Three tricolors drape the long bar. All eyes
are on red, white, blue balloons, the dim lights
colored to match. It's France. A mural-sized picture
of Marianne's pinned to a wall. Her joy
is inciting us on to liberty. Who could be quiet?

Everyone is shouting or singing. Leave quiet
for the morning. We mean to cheer for the day
revolutionaries swarmed the streets in joy,
hope in their hearts, the future in their eyes.
But in this crowd glimpses of an older picture:
anxious men hide their faces from the lights,

kept low against the world outside. Bar lights,
turned on high, would make the room fall quiet.
Everyone's seen last week's newspaper picture—
the faces, mug shots of queers arrested that day,
beaten, finger printed, their desperate eyes
blinded by flash bulbs, any hope for joy

destroyed for them. But holidays are meant for joy.
Let Bastille's be bright as any Festival of Lights
or carnival. He sits in a corner, his dark eyes
looking my way. I talk too much. He's quiet.
I'm bold. He warns me tomorrow is a working day.
That's o.k. I know what he's saying. I get the picture.

His room's small, spare, plain. Not one picture.
A bare mattress on the floor. Why do I feel a joy
higher than a holiday's, sweeter than a birthday,
finer than getting what I'd wished for? The lights
are off, no music's playing. Bud's world's quiet,
as silent as he and I are, as close. His eyes,

black as his skin in the night, stare into my eyes.
We could be photographers snapping a picture
or shooting a film, watching, waiting, quiet,
skilled at our job, reliant on chance—the joy
of the sun's scattering clouds, out of darkness lights,
like torches burning in Bastille cells that day

when, long used to quiet, night, prisoners' eyes,
stunned, blinded by day, were unable to picture
the joy to come, bewildered by the liberators' lights.

AUTUMN RHYTHM

On the Met wall, the picture looked suspended
in air, as if its paint had been flung to the wind
to watch it dance on its own. Stravinsky's *Rite*,
I thought, or the endless tune of Bach's aria.
In the steady beat of the fall woods behind
my house I'd seen, heard it before: in branches,
leaves, broken, tossed by pummeling rain,
wind, the thrill of a sky ripped open to sun.
Or in our groping in the back of Deak's car
parked along a dark road by the lake, frantic
to touch, to kiss, to feel what had been forbidden
us so long, too young to speak, only gasps,
then the aftermath, the trip back to a world
that now everywhere throbbed like a Pollock.

TWO ROSES

Ten, I saw Toscanini conduct Verdi.
'Incandescent' is a grownup's word,
but it's what I heard: his pulse fiery,
strict, alive to each heart-pumping beat.
As a child, I was electrified, charged.
I couldn't know he hid in a pocket
a handkerchief rose red with his mistress's
menses he'd smell before each concert.
Maybe, like poetry or music, fucking is
a way the undulating universe is enjoyed.
No sun throbs higher than a summer sky's.
Love takes its measure, colors all. Before,
your sex is dawn pink. After, sunset red,
like a rose outside, brash in windless quiet.

BESTIARY

Snake. Heating its blood on a rock a step
off a fire trail near Tam's peak, its jewel-like
scales that night in our bed diamond strong.
Uncoiling, it slithers fast into our nest's dark.

Hawk. Seen from our window on Telegraph Hill.
Our African Gray squawks as it spirals above
the house, ravenous for rats, mice in alleys,
streets. Bird-eyed, too, we dive for the thrill.

Fish. Tahoe is baltic blue. We leap in, until,
cold to the bones, balls like stones, we race
toward a steaming hot tub, the habitat we're
born for, a hot spring's stream melting ice.

Gryphon. Wings to ride on, fantasies, lies,
stories that roar lion-like when you're gone.

BIBLE STORIES

Not brothers, Brother, though so mistook by others.
We lived as lovers seven unbloodied years.
It's blasphemy, I know. But suppose after Jahweh
had denied his offerings of grain, Cain persuaded
Abel to toss aside the knife that had sliced
so many innocent throats and feast with him.
Or, seeing no lamb or goat on Mount Moriah,
Isaac unbound the ropes that tied him and fled
into the desert, there to find Ishmael
at home in lands the Old One didn't own.
Or Jesus, declared not guilty at his trial,
combing his fingers through James' hair, spared
nails, cross, spear, shocked to discover
no blood need be shed to love the world.

NEW YEAR'S DAY

Rounding the corner out of the park onto
the Great Highway, our dog and I magically
are trapped by the St. Ignatius track team
sprinting toward the ruins of the Sutro baths.

The mist is sun-lit, the Pacific mottled, sod green,
brown, streaked yellow—like the seaweed it tossed
ashore last night while you lay sleeping, softly
snoring, Nora's snout resting on your thigh.

Despite the streetlights' shining through our shades,
to restless eyes sometimes our house is so dark
it's impossible to see on which side of its doors—
ahead, behind—God is hiding. The future, I mean:
new worlds to be seen, lives to be revealed,
unheard words said, love still more surprising.

RITCH STREET BATHS

This night the boy god needs neither
ivy, wine, panther, pard, frenzied
women nor earthquake to break
free of you, just his old tricks

of the prick: quick as that,
imprisoned becomes imprisoner,
and you're as good as locked
in a room small as a jail cell,

its windowless walls barracks gray,
lying on a metal bed covered by
a sheet bleached threadbare
beneath an olive drab army

surplus blanket, a filthy speckled
basin sitting under a leaky roof
and a blue-tinted bulb dangling
as if about to drop from a cord,

your royal face, my lord, disguised
by darkness like a soldier's smudged
with soot for night patrol, your only clothes
a towel wrapped round your waist

like a loincloth the boy god with the golden
locks you're waiting for will strip off
like the chains he put on your wrists.
So freed, imprisoned becomes imprisoner

again, the bars you ordered are back
in place, and the seed you spill on
his sweating flesh is scattered like dragon's
teeth on Thebes, warriors for the kill.

JUNE HEAVY RAIN

Shower door open, you're rinsing off, scrubbing
your butt with your moving man's calloused hands.
I'm watching from the hall. Even after it's been
satisfied, desire's desire. Looking at you, I'm a kid
again, lost in a forest I thought I knew well,
scared bedtime dark will come with me not home.

Ricky's ill with polio. It's too wet for Mack's
mom to let him play. Through a clouded window,
gnarled wisteria, thrashing butterfly bush,
I watch rain gushing down a slide, pitting
a sandbox, bouncing off my rabbit hutch. His coat
like mud spattered hide stretched on a line
between two oak, a sick mule kicks, kicks at
the fence that keeps it from the battered woods.

TRENT KELLEY

HIDDEN IN THE OPEN

TRENT KELLEY is the author of "Ballad of a Long Hot Night" (a one-act drama) for TSI/Playtime Series. The play was produce in New York in February 2007. He is also the curator of "Hidden in the Open: A Photographic Essay of Afro American Male Couples," the name of a collection of photographs, one of which appears as the cover of Issue 07 of *Assaracus*. The photographs date from the mid-19th to the late-20th centuries. The title for this collection of photographs refers to gay men of African descent who generally participated in their larger ethnic community out in the open but with their same-sex affectionate relationships known only to those who knew them, such as close friends and family. By any other name or label, gay pride existed and was often recorded by gay men irrespective of race long before the liberating Stonewall Riots in 1969.

www.flickr.com/photos/hidden-in-the-open/

SUBMIT TO ASSARACUS

The mission of Sibling Rivalry Press is to develop, publish, and promote outlaw artistic talent—those projects which inspire people to read, challenge, and ponder the complexities of life in dark rooms, under blankets by cell-phone illumination, in the backseats of cars, and on spring-day park benches next to people reading Tennessee Williams. We encourage submissions to *Assaracus* by gay male poets of any age, regardless of background, education, or level of publication experience. Submissions are accepted during the months of January, May, and September. For more information, visit us online.

SUBSCRIBE TO ASSARACUS

Readers can subscribe to receive a year of *Assaracus*, one of *Library Journal*'s "Best New Magazines." The subscription price is $50.00 for U.S. readers and $80.00 for international readers (including shipping), which buys you four book-length (120+ pages), perfect-bound issues of our grand stage for gay contemporary poetry. Subscriptions are available through our website.

NEW FROM SIBLING RIVALRY PRESS

Skin Shift by Matthew Hittinger assembles a metamorphosis taxonomy in poems that spider spin, that nimbus twirl into Wonder Woman and leap with the Aboriginal kangaroo woman, that escape from a sub-trunk with Houdini and seduce like the Amazon's pink river dolphin man. Traditional forms morph into experimental narratives, lyrics, and dramatic monologues that present an invitation to slip inside the skins of others and to experience the mythologies that resonate in modern times. Says Mary Biddinger, author of *Saint Monica* and *Prairie Fever*, "Matthew Hittinger's poems have all the cool of an exquisitely-chiseled statue, but the blood that charges through their veins is pure hot glory."

www.siblingrivalrypress.com